YOKE

Cast on 49 sts **loosely**.
Rows 1-4: Knit across.
Row 5: K1, ★ P3, K1; repeat from ★ across.
Row 6 (Right side): P1, ★ K1, (YO, K1) twice, P1; repeat from ★ across: 73 sts.
Note: Loop a short piece of yarn through any stitch to mark last row as **right** side.
Row 7: K1, ★ P5, K1; repeat from ★ across.
Row 8: P1, ★ K5, P1; repeat from ★ across.
Row 9: K1, ★ P5, K1; repeat from ★ across.
Row 10: P1, ★ K2, YO, K1, YO, K2, P1; repeat from ★ across: 97 sts.
Row 11: K1, ★ P7, K1; repeat from ★ across.
Row 12: P1, ★ K7, P1; repeat from ★ across.
Row 13: K1, ★ P7, K1; repeat from ★ across.
Row 14: P1, ★ K3, YO, K1, YO, K3, P1; repeat from ★ across: 121 sts.
Row 15: K1, ★ P9, K1; repeat from ★ across.
Row 16: P1, ★ K9, P1; repeat from ★ across.
Row 17: K1, ★ P9, K1; repeat from ★ across.
Row 18: P1, ★ K4, YO, K1, YO, K4, P1; repeat from ★ across: 145 sts.
Row 19: K1, ★ P 11, K1; repeat from ★ across.
Row 20: P1, ★ K 11, P1; repeat from ★ across.
Row 21: K1, P 11, ★ knit into the front **and** into the back of the next st, P 11; repeat from ★ across to last st, K1: 156 sts.
Row 22: K1, YO, slip 1, K1, PSSO, K7, K2 tog, YO, ★ K2, YO, slip 1, K1, PSSO, K7, K2 tog, YO; repeat from ★ across to last st, K1.
Row 23: K2, P9, ★ K4, P9; repeat from ★ across to last 2 sts, K2.
Row 24: K2, YO, slip 1, K1, PSSO, K5, K2 tog, YO, ★ K4, YO, slip 1, K1, PSSO, K5, K2 tog, YO; repeat from ★ across to last 2 sts, K2.
Row 25: Purl across.
Row 26: K3, YO, slip 1, K1, PSSO, K3, K2 tog, YO, ★ K6, YO, slip 1, K1, PSSO, K3, K2 tog, YO; repeat from ★ across to last 3 sts, K3.
Row 27: K4, P5, ★ K8, P5; repeat from ★ across to last 4 sts, K4.
Row 28: K4, YO, slip 1, K1, PSSO, K1, K2 tog, YO, ★ K8, YO, slip 1, K1, PSSO, K1, K2 tog, YO; repeat from ★ across to last 4 sts, K4.
Row 29: Purl across.
Row 30: K5, YO, slip 1, K2 tog, PSSO, YO, ★ K 10, YO, slip 1, K2 tog, PSSO, YO; repeat from ★ across to last 5 sts, K5.
Rows 31 and 32: Knit across.
Row 33: Purl across.
Row 34: K2 tog twice, YO, (K1, YO) 5 times, ★ K2 tog 4 times, YO, (K1, YO) 5 times; repeat from ★ across to last 4 sts, K2 tog twice: 180 sts.
Rows 35 and 36: Knit across.
Row 37: Purl across.
Row 38: K2 tog twice, YO, (K1, YO) 7 times, ★ K2 tog 4 times, YO, (K1, YO) 7 times; repeat from ★ across to last 4 sts, K2 tog twice: 228 sts.
Rows 39 and 40: Knit across.
Row 41: Purl across.
Row 42: K2 tog 3 times, YO, (K1, YO) 7 times, ★ K2 tog 6 times, YO, (K1, YO) 7 times; repeat from ★ across to last 6 sts, K2 tog 3 times: 252 sts.
Rows 43 and 44: Knit across.
Row 45: Purl across.
Row 46: K2 tog 3 times, YO, (K1, YO) 9 times, ★ K2 tog 6 times, YO, (K1, YO) 9 times; repeat from ★ across to last 6 sts, K2 tog 3 times: 300 sts.
Rows 47 and 48: Knit across.
Row 49: Purl across.

Row 50: K2 tog 4 times, YO, (K1, YO) 9 times, ★ K2 ___ ___ ___ YO, (K1, YO) ___ ___ ___ ★
across ___
Rows ___
Row 5 ___
Row 5 ___
★ K2 ___
across ___

SKIRT

Rows 1 and 2: Knit across.
Dress Only - Row 3: P 62, bind off 62 sts **loosely**, P 123, bind off 62 sts **loosely**, purl across: 248 sts.
Gown Only - Row 3: P 124, slip 62 sts just worked onto st holder (Sleeve), P 186, slip 62 sts just worked onto second st holder (Sleeve), P 62: 248 sts.
Dress or Gown - Row 4: K2 tog 5 times, YO, (K1, YO) 11 times, ★ K2 tog 10 times, YO, (K1, YO) 11 times; repeat from ★ across to last 10 sts, K2 tog 5 times: 264 sts.
Rows 5 and 6: Knit across.
Row 7: Purl across.
Row 8: K2 tog 5 times, K1, (YO, K1) 12 times, ★ K2 tog 10 times, K1, (YO, K1) 12 times; repeat from ★ across to last 10 sts, K2 tog 5 times: 280 sts.
Rows 9 and 10: Knit across.
Row 11: Purl across.
Row 12: K2 tog 6 times, YO, (K1, YO) 11 times, ★ K2 tog 12 times, YO, (K1, YO) 11 times; repeat from ★ across to last 12 sts, K2 tog 6 times.
Rows 13 and 14: Knit across.
Repeat Rows 11-14 until Dress measures approximately 9(10-11)" **or** Gown measures approximately 18(19-20)" from cast on edge **or to desired length**, ending by working Row 14. Bind off all sts **loosely**.

SLEEVES - Gown Only

With **right** side facing, slip 62 sts from st holder onto needle.
Row 1: K2 tog 5 times, YO, (K1, YO) 11 times, K2 tog 10 times, YO, (K1, YO) 11 times, K2 tog 5 times: 66 sts.
Rows 2 and 3: Knit across.
Row 4: Purl across.
Row 5: K2 tog 5 times, K1, (YO, K1) 12 times, K2 tog 10 times, K1, (YO, K1) 12 times, K2 tog 5 times: 70 sts.
Rows 6 and 7: Knit across.
Row 8: Purl across.
Row 9: K2 tog 6 times, YO, (K1, YO) 11 times, K2 tog 12 times, YO, (K1, YO) 11 times, K2 tog 6 times.
Rows 10 and 11: Knit across.
Rows 12-23: Repeat Rows 8-11, 3 times.
Bind off all sts **loosely**.
Sew Sleeve seam.
Repeat for second Sleeve.

FINISHING

Sew back seam, leaving a 3″ neck opening.
EDGING
With **wrong** side facing, join yarn with slip st to top left back neck opening.
Row 1: Sc evenly spaced down left side and up right side.
Row 2: Ch 3, turn; skip first 2 sc, sc in next sc (button loop made), sc in each sc across; finish off.
Add button.

SACQUE to Knit

Size: Newborn, 3 months and 6 months

Note: Yarn amounts and Gauge are given for Newborn, with 3 months and 6 months in parentheses. Proper measurement is obtained by using different needle sizes as recommended under Materials.

MATERIALS
Baby Yarn, approximately:
  2(2¼-2½) ounces,
    [60(65-70) grams, 350(395-440) yards]
For Newborn size ONLY: 24″ Circular needle, size 3 (3.25 mm) **or** size needed for gauge
For 3 months size ONLY: 24″ Circular needle, size 4 (3.50 mm) **or** size needed for gauge
For 6 months size ONLY: 24″ Circular needle, size 5 (3.75 mm) **or** size needed for gauge
2 Stitch holders
3 Buttons

GAUGE: 1 Pattern (35 sts) = 3(3¼-3½)″
        26 rows = 2¼(2½-2¾)″
Work Gauge Swatch as follows:
Cast on 35 sts **very loosely**.
Rows 1 and 2: Knit across.
Row 3: Purl across.
Row 4: K2 tog 6 times, YO, (K1, YO) 11 times, K2 tog 6 times.
Rows 5-24: Repeat Rows 1-4, 5 times.
Rows 25 and 26: Knit across.
Bind off all sts **loosely**.

YOKE
Cast on 55 sts **loosely**.
Rows 1 and 2: Knit across.
Row 3 (Buttonhole row): K1, K2 tog, YO, knit across.
Rows 4-6: Knit across.
Row 7: K4, P3, ★ K1, P3; repeat from ★ across to last 4 sts, K4.
Row 8 (Right side): K3, P1, ★ K1, (YO, K1) twice, P1; repeat from ★ across to last 3 sts, K3: 79 sts.
Note: Loop a short piece of yarn through any stitch to mark last row as **right** side.
Row 9: K4, P5, ★ K1, P5; repeat from ★ across to last 4 sts, K4.
Row 10: K3, P1, ★ K5, P1; repeat from ★ across to last 3 sts, K3.
Row 11: K4, P5, ★ K1, P5; repeat from ★ across to last 4 sts, K4.
Row 12: K3, P1, ★ K2, YO, K1, YO, K2, P1; repeat from ★ across to last 3 sts, K3: 103 sts.
Row 13: K4, P7, ★ K1, P7; repeat from ★ across to last 4 sts, K4.
Row 14: K3, P1, ★ K7, P1; repeat from ★ across to last 3 sts, K3.
Row 15 (Buttonhole row): K1, K2 tog, YO, ★ K1, P7; repeat from ★ across to last 4 sts, K4.
Row 16: K3, P1, ★ K3, YO, K1, YO, K3, P1; repeat from ★ across to last 3 sts, K3: 127 sts.
Row 17: K4, P9, ★ K1, P9; repeat from ★ across to last 4 sts, K4.
Row 18: K3, P1, ★ K9, P1; repeat from ★ across to last 3 sts, K3.
Row 19: K4, P9, ★ K1, P9; repeat from ★ across to last 4 sts, K4.
Row 20: K3, P1, ★ K4, YO, K1, YO, K4, P1; repeat from ★ across to last 3 sts, K3: 151 sts.
Row 21: K4, P 11, ★ K1, P 11; repeat from ★ across to last 4 sts, K4.
Row 22: K3, P1, ★ K 11, P1; repeat from ★ across to last 3 sts, K3.
Row 23: K4, P 11, ★ knit into the front **and** into the back of the next st, P 11; repeat from ★ across to last 4 sts, K4: 162 sts.
Row 24: K4, YO, slip 1, K1, PSSO, K7, K2 tog, YO, ★ K2, YO, slip 1, K1, PSSO, K7, K2 tog, YO; repeat from ★ across to last 4 sts, K4.
Row 25: K5, P9, ★ K4, P9; repeat from ★ across to last 5 sts, K5.
Row 26: K5, YO, slip 1, K1, PSSO, K5, K2 tog, YO, ★ K4, YO, slip 1, K1, PSSO, K5, K2 tog, YO; repeat from ★ across to last 5 sts, K5.
Row 27: K3, purl across to last 3 sts, K3.
Row 28: K6, YO, slip 1, K1, PSSO, K3, K2 tog, YO, ★ K6, YO, slip 1, K1, PSSO, K3, K2 tog, YO; repeat from ★ across to last 6 sts, K6.
Row 29 (Buttonhole row): K1, K2 tog, YO, K4, P5, ★ K8, P5; repeat from ★ across to last 7 sts, K7.
Row 30: K7, YO, slip 1, K1, PSSO, K1, K2 tog, YO, ★ K8, YO, slip 1, K1, PSSO, K1, K2 tog, YO; repeat from ★ across to last 7 sts, K7.
Row 31: K3, purl across to last 3 sts, K3.
Row 32: K8, YO, slip 1, K2 tog, PSSO, YO, ★ K 10, YO, slip 1, K2 tog, PSSO, YO; repeat from ★ across to last 8 sts, K8.
Rows 33 and 34: Knit across.
Row 35: K3, purl across to last 3 sts, K3.
Row 36: K3, K2 tog twice, YO, (K1, YO) 5 times, ★ K2 tog 4 times, YO, (K1, YO) 5 times; repeat from ★ across to last 7 sts, K2 tog twice, K3: 186 sts.
Rows 37 and 38: Knit across.
Row 39: K3, purl across to last 3 sts, K3.

Row 40: K3, K2 tog twice, YO, (K1, YO) 7 times,
★ K2 tog 4 times, YO, (K1, YO) 7 times; repeat from ★
across to last 7 sts, K2 tog twice, K3: 234 sts.
Rows 41 and 42: Knit across.
Row 43: K3, purl across to last 3 sts, K3.
Row 44: K3, K2 tog 3 times, YO, (K1, YO) 7 times,
★ K2 tog 6 times, YO, (K1, YO) 7 times; repeat from ★
across to last 9 sts, K2 tog 3 times, K3: 258 sts.
Rows 45 and 46: Knit across.
Row 47: K3, purl across to last 3 sts, K3.
Row 48: K3, K2 tog 3 times, YO, (K1, YO) 9 times,
★ K2 tog 6 times, YO, (K1, YO) 9 times; repeat from ★
across to last 9 sts, K2 tog 3 times, K3: 306 sts.
Rows 49 and 50: Knit across.
Row 51: K3, purl across to last 3 sts, K3.
Row 52: K3, K2 tog 4 times, YO, (K1, YO) 9 times,
★ K2 tog 8 times, YO, (K1, YO) 9 times; repeat from ★
across to last 11 sts, K2 tog 4 times, K3: 330 sts.
Rows 53 and 54: Knit across.
Row 55: K3, purl across to last 3 sts, K3.
Row 56: K3, K2 tog 4 times, YO, (K1, YO) 11 times,
★ K2 tog 8 times, YO, (K1, YO) 11 times; repeat from ★
across to last 11 sts, K2 tog 4 times, K3: 378 sts.

BODY

Rows 1 and 2: Knit across.
Row 3: K3, P 124, slip 62 sts just worked onto st holder
(Sleeve), P 186, slip 62 sts just worked onto second st holder
(Sleeve), P 62, K3: 254 sts.
Row 4: K3, K2 tog 5 times, YO, (K1, YO) 11 times,
★ K2 tog 10 times, YO, (K1, YO) 11 times; repeat from ★
across to last 13 sts, K2 tog 5 times, K3: 270 sts.
Rows 5 and 6: Knit across.
Row 7: K3, purl across to last 3 sts, K3.
Row 8: K3, K2 tog 5 times, K1, (YO, K1) 12 times,
★ K2 tog 10 times, K1, (YO, K1) 12 times; repeat from ★
across to last 13 sts, K2 tog 5 times, K3: 286 sts.
Rows 9 and 10: Knit across.
Row 11: K3, purl across to last 3 sts, K3.
Row 12: K3, K2 tog 6 times, YO, (K1, YO) 11 times,
★ K2 tog 12 times, YO, (K1, YO) 11 times; repeat from ★
across to last 15 sts, K2 tog 6 times, K3.
Rows 13 and 14: Knit across.
Rows 15-18: Repeat Rows 11-14.
Bind off all sts **loosely**.
Add buttons.

SLEEVES

Work same as Gown, page 2.

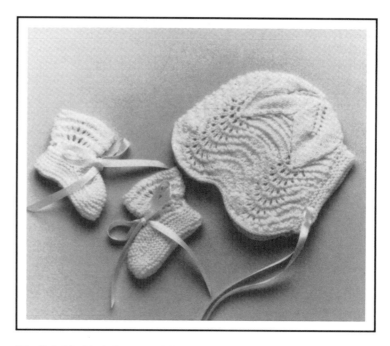

BONNET to Knit

Size: Newborn, 3 months and 6 months

Note: Yarn amounts and Gauge are given for Newborn, with
3 months and 6 months in parentheses. Proper measurement
is obtained by using different needle sizes as recommended
under Materials.

MATERIALS

Baby Yarn, approximately:
  ¾(1-1¼) ounces, [20(30-40) grams, 130(175-220) yards]
For Newborn size ONLY: Straight knitting needles,
  size 3 (3.25 mm) **or** size needed for gauge
For 3 months size ONLY: Straight knitting needles,
  size 4 (3.50 mm) **or** size needed for gauge
For 6 months size ONLY: Straight knitting needles,
  size 5 (3.75 mm) **or** size needed for gauge
¼" Ribbon - 1 yard

GAUGE: 1 Pattern (35 sts) = 3(3¼-3½)"
             26 rows = 2¼(2½-2¾)"
Work Gauge Swatch as follows:
Cast on 35 sts **very loosely**.
Rows 1 and 2: Knit across.
Row 3: Purl across.
Row 4: K2 tog 6 times, YO, (K1, YO) 11 times,
K2 tog 6 times.
Rows 5-24: Repeat Rows 1-4, 5 times.
Rows 25 and 26: Knit across.
Bind off all sts **loosely**.

Cast on 17 sts **loosely**.
Row 1: Purl across.
Row 2 (Right side): P1, ★ K1, (YO, K1) twice, P1; repeat from ★ across: 25 sts.
Note: Loop a short piece of yarn through any stitch to mark last row as **right** side.
Row 3: K1, ★ P5, K1; repeat from ★ across.
Row 4: P1, ★ K2, YO, K1, YO, K2, P1; repeat from ★ across: 33 sts.
Row 5: K1, ★ P7, K1; repeat from ★ across.
Row 6: P1, ★ K3, YO, K1, YO, K3, P1; repeat from ★ across: 41 sts.
Row 7: K1, ★ P9, K1; repeat from ★ across.
Row 8: P1, ★ K4, YO, K1, YO, K4, P1; repeat from ★ across: 49 sts.
Row 9: K1, ★ P 11, K1; repeat from ★ across.
Row 10: P1, ★ K5, YO, K1, YO, K5, P1; repeat from ★ across: 57 sts.
Row 11: K1, ★ P 13, K1; repeat from ★ across.
Row 12: P1, ★ K6, YO, K1, YO, K6, P1; repeat from ★ across: 65 sts.
Row 13: K1, ★ P 15, K1; repeat from ★ across.
Row 14: P1, ★ K7, YO, K1, YO, K7, P1; repeat from ★ across: 73 sts.
Row 15: K1, P 17, ★ knit into the front **and** into the back of the next st, P 17; repeat from ★ across to last st, K1: 76 sts. Place marker at each end of last row.
Row 16: K1, YO, slip 1, K1, PSSO, K 13, K2 tog, YO, ★ K2, YO, slip 1, K1, PSSO, K 13, K2 tog, YO; repeat from ★ across to last st, K1.
Row 17: Purl across.
Row 18: K2, YO, slip 1, K1, PSSO, K 11, K2 tog, YO, ★ K4, YO, slip 1, K1, PSSO, K 11, K2 tog, YO; repeat from ★ across to last 2 sts, K2.
Row 19: K3, P 13, ★ K6, P 13; repeat from ★ across to last 3 sts, K3.
Row 20: K3, YO, slip 1, K1, PSSO, K9, K2 tog, YO, ★ K6, YO, slip 1, K1, PSSO, K9, K2 tog, YO; repeat from ★ across to last 3 sts, K3.
Row 21: Purl across.
Row 22: K4, YO, slip 1, K1, PSSO, K7, K2 tog, YO, ★ K8, YO, slip 1, K1, PSSO, K7, K2 tog, YO; repeat from ★ across to last 4 sts, K4.
Row 23: K5, P9, ★ K 10, P9; repeat from ★ across to last 5 sts, K5.
Row 24: K5, YO, slip 1, K1, PSSO, K5, K2 tog, YO, ★ K 10, YO, slip 1, K1, PSSO, K5, K2 tog, YO; repeat from ★ across to last 5 sts, K5.
Row 25: Purl across.
Row 26: K6, YO, slip 1, K1, PSSO, K3, K2 tog, YO, ★ K 12, YO, slip 1, K1, PSSO, K3, K2 tog, YO; repeat from ★ across to last 6 sts, K6.
Row 27: K7, P5, ★ K 14, P5; repeat from ★ across to last 7 sts, K7.
Row 28: K7, YO, slip 1, K1, PSSO, K1, K2 tog, YO, ★ K 14, YO, slip 1, K1, PSSO, K1, K2 tog, YO; repeat from ★ across to last 7 sts, K7.
Row 29: Purl across.
Row 30: K8, YO, slip 1, K2 tog, PSSO, YO, ★ K 16, YO, slip 1, K2 tog, PSSO, YO; repeat from ★ across to last 8 sts, K8.
Rows 31 and 32: Knit across.
Row 33: Purl across.
Row 34: K2 tog 3 times, YO, (K1, YO) 7 times, ★ K2 tog 6 times, YO, (K1, YO) 7 times; repeat from ★ across to last 6 sts, K2 tog 3 times: 84 sts.
Rows 35 and 36: Knit across.
Row 37: Purl across.
Row 38: K2 tog 3 times, YO, (K1, YO) 9 times, ★ K2 tog 6 times, YO, (K1, YO) 9 times; repeat from ★ across to last 6 sts, K2 tog 3 times: 100 sts.

Rows 39 and 40: Knit across.
Row 41: Purl across.
Row 42: K2 tog 4 times, YO, (K1, YO) 9 times, ★ K2 tog 8 times, YO, (K1, YO) 9 times; repeat from ★ across to last 8 sts, K2 tog 4 times: 108 sts.
Rows 43 and 44: Knit across.
Row 45: Purl across.
Row 46: K2 tog 4 times, YO, (K1, YO) 11 times, ★ K2 tog 8 times, YO, (K1, YO) 11 times; repeat from ★ across to last 8 sts, K2 tog 4 times: 124 sts.
Rows 47 and 48: Knit across.
Row 49: Purl across.
Row 50: K2 tog 5 times, YO, (K1, YO) 11 times, ★ K2 tog 10 times, YO, (K1, YO) 11 times; repeat from ★ across to last 10 sts, K2 tog 5 times: 132 sts.
Rows 51 and 52: Knit across.
Row 53: Purl across.
Row 54: K2 tog 5 times, K1, (YO, K1) 12 times, ★ K2 tog 10 times, K1, (YO, K1) 12 times; repeat from ★ across to last 10 sts, K2 tog 5 times: 140 sts.
Rows 55 and 56: Knit across.
Row 57: Purl across.
Row 58: K2 tog 6 times, YO, (K1, YO) 11 times, ★ K2 tog 12 times, YO, (K1, YO) 11 times; repeat from ★ across to last 12 sts, K2 tog 6 times.
Row 59: Knit across.
Row 60: ★ K2, K2 tog; repeat from ★ across: 105 sts.
Bind off all sts **loosely**.

FINISHING

Weave yarn through cast on stitches; draw up tightly.
Sew back seam to markers.
NECK BAND
With **right** side facing, pick up 50 sts evenly spaced across neck edge *(Fig. 1b, page 1)*.
Rows 1-5: Knit across.
Bind off all sts **loosely**.
Sew on Ribbon for ties using photo as a guide for placement.

BOOTIES to Knit

Size: Newborn, 3 months and 6 months

Note: Yarn amounts and Gauge are given for Newborn, with 3 months and 6 months in parentheses. Proper measurement is obtained by using different needle sizes as recommended under Materials.

MATERIALS
Baby Yarn, approximately:
½(¾-1) ounce, [15(20-30) grams, 90(130-175) yards]
For Newborn size ONLY: Straight knitting needles, size 3 (3.25 mm) **or** size needed for gauge
For 3 months size ONLY: Straight knitting needles, size 4 (3.50 mm) **or** size needed for gauge
For 6 months size ONLY: Straight knitting needles, size 5 (3.75 mm) **or** size needed for gauge
2 Stitch holders
¼″ Ribbon - 1 yard

GAUGE: 1 Pattern (35 sts) = 3(3¼-3½)"
    26 rows = 2¼(2½-2¾)"
Work Gauge Swatch as follows:
Cast on 35 sts **very loosely.**
Rows 1 and 2: Knit across.
Row 3: Purl across.
Row 4: K2 tog 6 times, YO, (K1, YO) 11 times,
K2 tog 6 times.
Rows 5-24: Repeat Rows 1-4, 5 times.
Rows 25 and 26: Knit across.
Bind off all sts **loosely.**

CUFF

Cast on 30 sts **loosely.**
Row 1 (Right side)**:** Knit across.
Note: Loop a short piece of yarn through any stitch to mark
last row as **right** side.
Row 2 (Eyelet row)**:** K2, ★ YO, K2 tog; repeat from ★
across.
Rows 3-5: Knit across.
Row 6: Purl across.
Row 7: K2 tog twice, YO, (K1, YO) 7 times, K2 tog 4 times,
YO, (K1, YO) 7 times, K2 tog twice: 38 sts.
Rows 8 and 9: Knit across.
Row 10: Purl across.
Row 11: K2 tog 3 times, YO, (K1, YO) 7 times,
K2 tog 6 times, YO, (K1, YO) 7 times, K2 tog 3 times: 42 sts.
Rows 12 and 13: Knit across.
Row 14: Purl across.
Row 15: K2 tog 4 times, YO, (K1, YO) 5 times,
K2 tog 8 times, YO, (K1, YO) 5 times, K2 tog 4 times: 38 sts.
Rows 16 and 17: Knit across.
Bind off all sts **loosely.**

INSTEP

With **right** side facing, pick up 30 sts along cast on edge
(Fig. 1a, page 1).
Row 1 (Wrong side)**:** Knit across.
Row 2: K 20, slip remaining 10 sts onto st holder: 20 sts.
Row 3: K 10, slip remaining 10 sts onto second st holder:
10 sts.
Rows 4-23: Knit across; at end of last row, cut yarn.

SIDES

Row 1: With **right** side facing, slip sts from st holder onto
empty needle, pick up 10 sts along right side of Instep
(Fig. 1b, page 1), K 10, pick up 10 sts along left side of
Instep, slip sts from st holder onto empty needle, knit across:
50 sts.
Rows 2-12: Knit across.
Row 13: K3, K2 tog, K 15, K2 tog, K6, K2 tog, K 15,
K2 tog, K3: 46 sts.
Row 14: Knit across.
Bind off all sts.

FINISHING

Sew seam.
Weave Ribbon through Eyelet row.

BLANKET to Knit

Size: Approximately 31" x 31"

MATERIALS
    Baby Yarn, approximately:
        11 ounces, (310 grams, 1,925 yards)
    24" Circular knitting needle, size 7 (4.50 mm) **or** size
    needed for gauge

Note: Entire Blanket is worked holding two strands of yarn
together.

GAUGE: Working double strand, 2 Patterns (34 sts) = 6"
    27 Rows = 3½"
Work Gauge Swatch as follows:
Cast on 34 sts **very loosely.**
Rows 1-3: Knit across.
Row 4: Purl across.
Row 5: K2 tog 3 times, YO, (K1, YO) 5 times,
K2 tog 6 times, YO, (K1, YO) 5 times, K2 tog 3 times.
Rows 6 and 7: Knit across.
Rows 8-27: Repeat Rows 4-7, 5 times.
Bind off all sts **loosely.**

Cast on 176 sts **very loosely.**
Rows 1-3: Knit across.
Row 4: K3, purl across to last 3 sts, K3.
Row 5: K3, K2 tog 3 times, YO, (K1, YO) 5 times,
★ K2 tog 6 times, YO, (K1, YO) 5 times; repeat from ★
across to last 9 sts, K2 tog 3 times, K3.
Rows 6 and 7: Knit across.
Repeat Rows 4-7 until Blanket measures approximately 31" **or**
to desired length, ending by working Row 7.
Bind off all sts **loosely.**

DRESS OR GOWN to Crochet

Size: Newborn to 3 months and 4 to 6 months

Size Note: Instructions are written for Newborn to 3 months with 4 to 6 months in parentheses.

MATERIALS
Baby Yarn, approximately:
   Dress - 2½(2¾) ounces, [70(80) grams, 440(480) yards]
   Gown - 5(5½) ounces, [140(160) grams, 875(965) yards]
Size 8 Pearl Cotton (for Edging), approximately 30 yards
Crochet hook, size D (3.00 mm) **or** size needed for gauge
2 Buttons
¼″ Ribbon - 1¼ yards (For Gown Only)

GAUGE: (7 dc, Shell) twice = 4″

YOKE

Ch 59 **loosely**.
Row 1 (Right side): [(2 Dc, ch 2, 2 dc) in fifth ch from hook **(Shell made)**], skip next ch, dc in next ch, ★ skip next ch, work Shell in next ch, skip next ch, dc in next ch; repeat from ★ across: 14 Shells.
Note: Loop a short piece of yarn through any stitch to mark last row as **right** side.
Row 2: Ch 3 **(counts as first dc, now and throughout)**, turn; work Shell in first ch-2 sp, ★ skip next dc, dc in next 2 dc, work Shell in next ch-2 sp; repeat from ★ across to last 3 dc, skip next 2 dc, dc in last dc.
Row 3: Ch 3, turn; dc in next dc, work Shell in next ch-2 sp, ★ skip next dc, dc in next 3 dc, work Shell in next ch-2 sp; repeat from ★ across to last 3 dc, skip next dc, dc in last 2 dc.
Row 4: Ch 3, turn; dc in next dc, work Shell in next ch-2 sp, ★ skip next dc, dc in next 4 dc, work Shell in next ch-2 sp; repeat from ★ across to last 4 dc, skip 2 dc, dc in last 2 dc.

Row 5: Ch 3, turn; dc in next 2 dc, work Shell in next ch-2 sp, ★ skip next dc, dc in next 5 dc, work Shell in next ch-2 sp; repeat from ★ across to last 4 dc, skip next dc, dc in last 3 dc.
Row 6: Ch 3, turn; dc in next 2 dc, work Shell in next ch-2 sp, ★ skip next dc, dc in next 6 dc, work Shell in next ch-2 sp; repeat from ★ across to last 5 dc, skip 2 dc, dc in last 3 dc.
Row 7: Ch 3, turn; dc in next 3 dc, work Shell in next ch-2 sp, ★ skip next dc, dc in next 7 dc, work Shell in next ch-2 sp; repeat from ★ across to last 5 dc, skip next dc, dc in last 4 dc.
Row 8: Ch 3, turn; dc in next 3 dc, work Shell in next ch-2 sp, ★ skip 2 dc, dc in next 7 dc, work Shell in next ch-2 sp; repeat from ★ across to last 6 dc, skip 2 dc, dc in last 4 dc.
Row 9: Ch 3, turn; dc in next 3 dc, work Shell in next ch-2 sp, ★ skip next dc, dc in next 8 dc, work Shell in next ch-2 sp; repeat from ★ across to last 6 dc, skip 2 dc, dc in last 4 dc.

Size Newborn to 3 months ONLY
Row 10: Ch 3, turn; dc in next 3 dc, work Shell in next ch-2 sp, skip 2 dc, dc in next 8 dc, † work Shell in next ch-2 sp, skip 2 dc, dc in next 4 dc, skip 3 ch-2 sps plus 6 dc (Armhole), dc in next 4 dc †, (work Shell in next ch-2 sp, skip 2 dc, dc in next 8 dc) 3 times, repeat from † to † once, work Shell in next ch-2 sp, skip 2 dc, dc in next 8 dc, work Shell in next ch-2 sp, skip 2 dc, dc in last 4 dc: 8 Shells.
Row 11: Ch 3, turn; dc in next 3 dc, work Shell in next ch-2 sp, ★ skip next dc, dc in next 9 dc, work Shell in next ch-2 sp; repeat from ★ across to last 6 dc, skip next dc, dc in last 5 dc; join with slip st to first dc.

Size 4 to 6 months ONLY
Row 10: Ch 3, turn; dc in next 3 dc, work Shell in next ch-2 sp, ★ skip 2 dc, dc in next 8 dc, work Shell in next ch-2 sp; repeat from ★ across to last 6 dc, skip 2 dc, dc in last 4 dc.
Row 11: Ch 3, turn; dc in next 4 dc, work Shell in next ch-2 sp, ★ skip next dc, dc in next 9 dc, work Shell in next ch-2 sp; repeat from ★ across to last 6 dc, skip next dc, dc in last 5 dc.
Row 12: Ch 3, turn; dc in next 4 dc, work Shell in next ch-2 sp, skip 2 dc, dc in next 9 dc, † work Shell in next ch-2 sp, skip 2 dc, dc in next 5 dc, skip 3 ch-2 sps plus 7 dc (Armhole), dc in next 4 dc †, (work Shell in next ch-2 sp, skip 2 dc, dc in next 9 dc) 3 times, repeat from † to † once, work Shell in next ch-2 sp, skip 2 dc, dc in next 9 dc, work Shell in next ch-2 sp, skip 2 dc, dc in last 5 dc; join with slip st to first dc: 8 Shells.

SKIRT

Rnd 1: Turn; slip st in first 3 dc, ch 3, dc in next 2 dc, work Shell in next ch-2 sp, skip 2 dc, dc in next 3 dc, skip next dc, work Shell in next dc, ★ skip next dc, dc in next 3 dc, work Shell in next ch-2 sp, skip 2 dc, dc in next 3 dc, skip next dc, work Shell in next dc; repeat from ★ around; join with slip st to first dc: 16 Shells.
Rnd 2: Ch 3, turn; work Shell in next ch-2 sp, ★ skip 2 dc, dc in next 3 dc, work Shell in next ch-2 sp; repeat from ★ around to last 4 dc, skip 2 dc, dc in last 2 dc; join with slip st to first dc.
Rnd 3: Ch 3, turn; dc in same st, dc in next 2 dc, work Shell in next ch-2 sp, ★ skip next dc, dc in next 4 dc, work Shell in next ch-2 sp; repeat from ★ around; join with slip st to first dc.

Rnd 4: Ch 3, turn; work Shell in next ch-2 sp, ★ skip 2 dc, dc in next 4 dc, work Shell in next ch-2 sp; repeat from ★ around to last 5 dc, skip 2 dc, dc in last 3 dc; join with slip st to first dc.

Rnd 5: Ch 3, turn; dc in next 3 dc, work Shell in next ch-2 sp, ★ skip 2 dc, dc in next 4 dc, work Shell in next ch-2 sp; repeat from ★ around; join with slip st to first dc.

Rnd 6: Ch 3, turn; work Shell in next ch-2 sp, ★ skip next dc, dc in next 5 dc, work Shell in next ch-2 sp; repeat from ★ around to last 5 dc, skip next dc, dc in last 4 dc; join with slip st to first dc.

Rnd 7: Ch 3, turn; dc in next 4 dc, work Shell in next ch-2 sp, ★ skip 2 dc, dc in next 5 dc, work Shell in next ch-2 sp; repeat from ★ around; join with slip st to first dc.

Rnd 8: Ch 3, turn; work Shell in next ch-2 sp, ★ skip 2 dc, dc in next 5 dc, work Shell in next ch-2 sp; repeat from ★ around to last 6 dc, skip 2 dc, dc in last 4 dc; join with slip st to first dc.

Rnd 9: Ch 3, turn; dc in same st, dc in next 4 dc, work Shell in next ch-2 sp, ★ skip next dc, dc in next 6 dc, work Shell in next ch-2 sp; repeat from ★ around; join with slip st to first dc.

Rnd 10: Ch 3, turn; work Shell in next ch-2 sp, ★ skip 2 dc, dc in next 6 dc, work Shell in next ch-2 sp; repeat from ★ around to last 7 dc, skip 2 dc, dc in last 5 dc; join with slip st to first dc.

Rnd 11: Ch 3, turn; dc in next 5 dc, work Shell in next ch-2 sp, ★ skip 2 dc, dc in next 6 dc, work Shell in next ch-2 sp; repeat from ★ around; join with slip st to first dc.

Rnd 12: Ch 3, turn; work Shell in next ch-2 sp, ★ skip next dc, dc in next 7 dc, work Shell in next ch-2 sp; repeat from ★ around to last 7 dc, skip next dc, dc in last 6 dc; join with slip st to first dc.

Rnd 13: Ch 3, turn; dc in next 6 dc, work Shell in next ch-2 sp, ★ skip 2 dc, dc in next 7 dc, work Shell in next ch-2 sp; repeat from ★ around; join with slip st to first dc.

Rnd 14: Ch 3, turn; work Shell in next ch-2 sp, ★ skip 2 dc, dc in next 7 dc, work Shell in next ch-2 sp; repeat from ★ around to last 8 dc, skip 2 dc, dc in last 6 dc; join with slip st to first dc.

Repeat Rnds 13 and 14 until Dress measures approximately 9½(11)″ **or** Gown measures approximately 18½(20)″ from beginning **or to desired length**; at end of last rnd, finish off.

SLEEVES

Rnd 1: With **wrong** side facing, join yarn with slip st in first skipped dc on Row 9(11) of Yoke, ch 3, dc in next 2 dc, work Shell in next ch-2 sp, skip 2 dc, ★ dc in next 7(8) dc, work Shell in next ch-2 sp, skip 2 dc; repeat from ★ once **more**, dc in last 4(5) dc; join with slip st to first dc.

Rnd 2: Ch 3, turn; dc in next 3(4) dc, work Shell in next ch-2 sp, skip 2 dc, ★ dc in next 6(7) dc, work Shell in next ch-2 sp, skip 2 dc; repeat from ★ once **more**, dc in last 2 dc; join with slip st to first dc.

Rnd 3: Ch 3, turn; dc in next dc, 4 dc in next ch-2 sp, skip 2 dc, ★ dc in next 5(6) dc, 4 dc in next ch-2 sp, skip 2 dc; repeat from ★ once **more**, dc in last 3(4) dc; join with slip st to first dc.

Rnd 4: Ch 1, turn; sc in each dc around; join with slip st to first sc, finish off.
Sew underarm opening.
Repeat for second Sleeve.

FINISHING

NECK EDGING

Size Newborn to 3 months ONLY - Rnd 1: With **right** side facing, join yarn with slip st at base of Yoke opening, work 22 sc evenly spaced along right front edge; working in free loops of beginning ch, (sc, ch 1, sc) in first ch, sc in next 3 chs, skip next ch, ★ sc in next 3 chs, skip next ch; repeat from ★ across to last 4 chs, sc in next 3 chs, (sc, ch 1, sc) in last ch; work 22 sc evenly spaced along left front edge; join with slip st to first sc, finish off.

Size 4 to 6 months ONLY - Rnd 1: With **right** side facing, join yarn with slip st at base of Yoke opening, work 24 sc evenly spaced along right front edge; working in free loops of beginning ch, (sc, ch 1, sc) in first ch, sc in each ch across to last ch, (sc, ch 1, sc) in last ch; work 24 sc evenly spaced along left front edge; join with slip st to first sc, finish off.

Both Sizes - Rnd 2: With **right** side facing, join pearl cotton with slip st in first sc, ch 1, sc in same st and in next 10(11) sc, ch 7, sc in same st, sc in next 11(12) sc, ch 7, sc in same st, sc in next sc, (sc, ch 1, sc) in ch-1 sp, sc in each sc across to ch-1 sp, (sc, ch 1, sc) in ch-1 sp, sc in each sc across; join with slip st to first sc, finish off.

SKIRT EDGING

With **right** side facing, join pearl cotton with slip st in dc before any Shell, ★ 9 dc in next ch-2 sp, skip 2 dc, slip st in next dc, skip 2 dc, 7 dc in next dc, skip 2 dc, slip st in next dc; repeat from ★ around; join with slip st to first st, finish off.

SLEEVE EDGING

With **right** side facing, join pearl cotton with slip st to any sc, ch 1, sc in same st and in each sc around; join with slip st to first sc, finish off.
Repeat for second Sleeve.

Add buttons.

For Gown ONLY: Weave Ribbon through last row of Yoke, tie in front.

SACQUE to Crochet

Size: Newborn to 3 months and 4 to 6 months

Size Note: Instructions are written for Newborn to 3 months with 4 to 6 months in parentheses.

MATERIALS
Baby Yarn, approximately:
  2(2¼) ounces, [60(65) grams, 350(395) yards]
Size 8 Pearl Cotton (for Edging), approximately 30 yards
Crochet hook, size D (3.00 mm) **or** size needed for gauge
3 Buttons

GAUGE: 6 dc = 1"

YOKE

Work same as Dress, page 9, through Row 10(12); do **not** join or finish off.

BODY

Row 1: Ch 3, turn; dc in next 3(4) dc, work Shell in next ch-2 sp, ★ skip 2 dc, dc in next 8(9) dc, work Shell in next ch-2 sp; repeat from ★ across to last 6(7) dc, skip 2 dc, dc in last 4(5) dc.
Row 2: Ch 3, turn; dc in next 4 dc, work Shell in next ch-2 sp, ★ skip 1(2) dc, dc in next 9 dc, work Shell in next ch-2 sp; repeat from ★ across to last 6(7) dc, skip 1(2) dc, dc in last 5 dc.
Row 3: Ch 3, turn; dc in next 4 dc, work Shell in next ch-2 sp, ★ skip 2(1) dc, dc in next 9(10) dc, work Shell in next ch-2 sp; repeat from ★ across to last 7 dc, skip 2 dc, dc in last 5 dc.
Row 4: Ch 3, turn; dc in next 4 dc, work Shell in next ch-2 sp, ★ skip 2 dc, dc in next 9(10) dc, work Shell in next ch-2 sp; repeat from ★ across to last 7 dc, skip 2 dc, dc in last 5 dc.
Row 5: Ch 3, turn; dc in next 4 dc, work Shell in next ch-2 sp, ★ skip 1(2) dc, dc in next 10 dc, work Shell in next ch-2 sp; repeat from ★ across to last 7 dc, skip 2 dc, dc in last 5 dc.

Row 6: Ch 3, turn; dc in next 4(5) dc, work Shell in next ch-2 sp, ★ skip 2(1) dc, dc in next 10(11) dc, work Shell in next ch-2 sp; repeat from ★ across to last 7 dc, skip 2(1) dc, dc in last 5(6) dc.
Row 7: Ch 3, turn; dc in next 4(5) dc, work Shell in next ch-2 sp, ★ skip 2 dc, dc in next 10(11) dc, work Shell in next ch-2 sp; repeat from ★ across to last 7(8) dc, skip 2 dc, dc in last 5(6) dc.
Row 8: Ch 3, turn; dc in next 5 dc, work Shell in next ch-2 sp, ★ skip next dc, dc in next 11(12) dc, work Shell in next ch-2 sp; repeat from ★ across to last 7(8) dc, skip 1(2) dc, dc in last 6 dc.
Rows 9 and 10: Ch 3, turn; dc in next 5 dc, work Shell in next ch-2 sp, ★ skip 2 dc, dc in next 11(12) dc, work Shell in next ch-2 sp; repeat from ★ across to last 8 dc, skip 2 dc, dc in last 6 dc; for Newborn to 3 months Only, finish off.

Size 4 to 6 months ONLY
Row 11: Ch 3, turn; dc in next 6 dc, work Shell in next ch-2 sp, ★ skip next dc, dc in next 13 dc, work Shell in next ch-2 sp; repeat from ★ across to last 8 dc, skip next dc, dc in last 7 dc.
Rows 12 and 13: Ch 3, turn; dc in next 6 dc, work Shell in next ch-2 sp, ★ skip 2 dc, dc in next 13 dc, work Shell in next ch-2 sp; repeat from ★ across to last 9 dc, skip 2 dc, dc in last 7 dc; at end of last row, finish off.

SLEEVES

Rnd 1: With **wrong** side facing, join yarn with slip st in first skipped dc on Row 9(11) of Yoke, ch 3, dc in next 3 dc, work Shell in next ch-2 sp, skip 2 dc, ★ dc in next 8(9) dc, work Shell in next ch-2 sp, skip 2 dc; repeat from ★ once **more**, dc in last 4(5) dc; join with slip st to first dc.
Rnd 2: Ch 3, turn; dc in next 4(5) dc, work Shell in next ch-2 sp, ★ skip 2 dc, dc in next 8(9) dc, work Shell in next ch-2 sp; repeat from ★ once **more**, dc in last 3 dc; join with slip st to first dc.
Rnd 3: Ch 3, turn; dc in next 3 dc, work Shell in next ch-2 sp, ★ skip 2 dc, dc in next 8(9) dc, work Shell in next ch-2 sp; repeat from ★ once **more**, dc in last 4(5) dc; join with slip st to first dc.
Repeat Rnds 2 and 3 until Sleeve measures approximately 6½(8½)" from beginning; at end of last rnd, finish off.
Sew underarm opening.
Repeat for second Sleeve.

FINISHING
RIGHT FRONT BAND
Row 1: With **right** side facing, join yarn with slip st in last dc on last row of Body, ch 1, working in ends of rows across right front edge, work 41(49) sc evenly spaced across.
Row 2 (Buttonhole row)**:** Ch 1, turn; sc in first sc, (ch 2, skip 2 sc, sc in next 7 sc) twice, ch 2, skip 2 sc, sc in each sc across.
Row 3: Ch 1, turn; (sc in each sc across to ch-2 sp, 2 sc in ch-2 sp) 3 times, (sc, ch 1, sc) in last sc; do **not** finish off.

NECK BAND
Size Newborn to 3 months ONLY: Sc in end of next 2 rows; working in free loops of beginning ch, skip first ch, (sc in next 3 chs, skip next ch) 13 times, sc in next 2 chs, (sc, ch 1, sc) in last ch; do **not** finish off.

Size 4 to 6 months ONLY: Sc in end of next 2 rows; working in free loops of beginning ch, sc in each ch across to last ch, (sc, ch 1, sc) in last ch; do **not** finish off.

LEFT FRONT BAND

Row 1: Working in ends of rows across left front edge, work 40(48) sc evenly spaced across.
Row 2: Ch 1, turn; sc in first 41(49) sc.
Row 3: Ch 1, turn; sc in each sc across.
Finishing Row: Ch 1, turn; sc in first 40(48) sc; (sc, ch 1, sc) in last sc, sc in ends of next 3 rows, sc in each sc across Neck Band to ch-1 sp, (sc, ch-1, sc) in ch-1 sp; sc in each sc across; finish off.

BODY EDGING

With **right** side facing, join pearl cotton with slip st in first dc of last row of Body, skip 2 dc, 7 dc in next dc, skip 2 dc, slip st in next dc, 9 dc in next ch-2 sp, ★ skip 1(2) dc, slip st in next dc, (skip 2 dc, 7 dc in next dc, skip 2 dc, slip st in next dc) twice, 9 dc in next ch-2 sp; repeat from ★ 6 times **more**, skip 1(2) dc, slip st in next dc, skip 2 dc, 7 dc in next dc, skip 2 dc, slip st in last dc, sc in end of each row of Right Front Band, (sc, ch 1, sc) in next sc; sc in each sc across Band to ch-1 sp, (sc, ch 1, sc) in ch-1 sp; sc in each sc across to ch-1 sp, (sc, ch 1, sc) in ch-1 sp; sc in each sc across Left Front Band to last sc, (sc, ch 1, sc) in last sc; sc in end of each row of Left Front Band; join with slip st to first st, finish off.

SLEEVE EDGING

With **right** side facing, join pearl cotton with slip st in dc before any Shell, ★ 9 dc in next ch-2 sp, skip 2 dc, slip st in next dc, skip 3 dc, 7 dc in next dc, skip 2(3) dc, slip st in next dc; repeat from ★ around; finish off.
Repeat for second Sleeve.

Add buttons.

BONNET to Crochet

Size: Newborn to 3 months and 4 to 6 months

Size Note: Instructions are written for Newborn to 3 months with 4 to 6 months in parentheses.

MATERIALS
Baby Yarn, approximately:
  ¾(1) ounce, [20(30) grams, 130(175) yards]
Size 8 Pearl Cotton (for Edging), approximately 7 yards
Crochet hook, size D (3.00 mm) **or** size needed for gauge
¼" Ribbon - 1 yard

GAUGE: [7(8) dc, Shell] twice = 4(4¼)"

BACK

Ch 4, join with slip st to form a ring.
Rnd 1: Work 8 hdc in ring.
Note #1: Back is worked in rounds without joining. Place a 2" scrap of yarn before the first stitch of each round, moving marker after each round is completed.
Note #2: Work in Back Loops Only throughout Back.
Rnd 2: 2 Hdc in each hdc around: 16 hdc.
Rnd 3: 2 Hdc in next hdc **(increase made)**, hdc in next hdc, ★ increase, hdc in next hdc; repeat from ★ around: 24 hdc.
Rnd 4: ★ Increase, hdc in next 2 hdc; repeat from ★ around: 32 hdc.
Rnd 5: ★ Increase, hdc in next 3 hdc; repeat from ★ around: 40 hdc.
Rnd 6: ★ Increase, hdc in next 4 hdc; repeat from ★ around: 48 hdc.
Rnd 7: ★ Increase, hdc in next 5 hdc; repeat from ★ around: 56 hdc.
Rnd 8: ★ Increase, hdc in next 6 hdc; repeat from ★ around: 64 hdc.
Rnd 9: ★ Increase, hdc in next 7 hdc; repeat from ★ around: 72 hdc.

Size 4 to 6 months ONLY - **Rnd 10:** ★ Increase, hdc in next 8 hdc; repeat from ★ around: 80 hdc.

CROWN

Row 1 (Right side): Working in **both** loops, slip st in next hdc, ch 3 **(counts as first dc, now and throughout)**, dc in next 6(7) hdc, ★ skip 2 hdc, [(2 dc, ch 2, 2 dc) in next hdc **(Shell made)**], skip 2 hdc, dc in next 7(8) hdc; repeat from ★ 4 times **more**, leave last 5(7) hdc unworked: 5 Shells.
Note: Loop a short piece of yarn through any stitch to mark last row as **right** side.
Row 2: Ch 3, turn; dc in next 6(7) dc, ★ work Shell in next ch-2 sp, skip 2 dc, dc in next 7(8) dc; repeat from ★ across.
Repeat Row 2, 8(9) times.

FRONT BAND

Row 1: Ch 1, turn; sc in first 8(9) dc, skip next dc, sc in next ch-2 sp, skip next dc, ★ sc in next 9(10) dc, skip next dc, sc in next ch-2 sp, skip next dc; repeat from ★ 3 times **more**, sc in last 8(9) dc: 57(63) sc.
Rows 2-4: Ch 1, turn; sc in each sc across.
Row 5: Ch 3, turn; dc in next 6(7) sc, ★ skip next sc, work Shell in next sc, skip next sc, dc in next 7(8) sc; repeat from ★ 4 times **more**.
Rows 6 and 7: Ch 3, turn; dc in next 6(7) dc, ★ work Shell in next ch-2 sp, skip 2 dc, dc in next 7(8) dc; repeat from ★ 4 times **more**; at end of last row, finish off.

FINISHING

EDGING
With **wrong** side facing, join pearl cotton with slip st in first dc, skip 2(3) dc, 7 dc in next dc, skip 2 dc, slip st in next dc, ★ 9 dc in next ch-2 sp, skip 2 dc, slip st in next dc, skip 2(3) dc, 7 dc in next dc, skip 2 dc, slip st in next dc; repeat from ★ 4 times **more**; finish off.

NECK BAND
Fold Front Band to outside along Row 4.
Row 1: With **right** side facing, join yarn with slip st at corner, work 5 sc evenly spaced through **both** thicknesses, work 18(20) sc evenly spaced across Crown edge, work 4(5) sc evenly spaced across Back, work 18(20) evenly spaced across Crown edge, work 5 sc evenly spaced through **both** thicknesses of Front Band: 50(55) sc.
Rows 2-4: Ch 1, turn; sc in each sc across; at end of last row, finish off.
Sew on Ribbon for ties using photo as a guide for placement.

BOOTIES to Crochet

Size: Newborn to 3 months and 4 to 6 months

Size Note: Instructions are written for Newborn to 3 months with 4 to 6 months in parentheses.

MATERIALS

Baby Yarn, approximately:
½(¾) ounce, [15(20) grams, 90(130) yards]
Size 8 Pearl Cotton (for Edging), approximately 4 yards
Crochet hook, size D (3.00 mm) **or** size needed for gauge
¼" Ribbon - 1 yard

GAUGE: (7 dc, Shell) twice = 4"

CUFF

Ch 34 **loosely.**
Row 1 (Right side): Dc in sixth ch from hook, ★ ch 1, skip next ch, dc in next ch; repeat from ★ across: 16 dc.
Note: Loop a short piece of yarn through any stitch to mark last row as **right** side.
Row 2: Ch 3 **(counts as first dc, now and throughout)**, turn; dc in first ch-1 sp, dc in next dc, dc in next ch-1 sp, [(2 dc, ch 2, 2 dc) in next ch-1 sp **(Shell made)]**, ★ dc in next ch-1 sp, (dc in next dc, dc in next ch-1 sp) 3 times, work Shell in next ch-1 sp; repeat from ★ once **more**, dc in next ch-1 sp, dc in next dc, 2 dc in ch-5 sp.
Row 3: Ch 3, turn; dc in next 3 dc, (work Shell in next ch-2 sp, skip 2 dc, dc in next 7 dc) twice, work Shell in next ch-2 sp, skip 2 dc, dc in last 4 dc.
Repeat Row 3, 2(3) times; at end of last row, finish off.

INSTEP

Row 1: With **right** side facing and working in free loops of beginning ch, join yarn with slip st in 12th ch, ch 1, sc in same st and in next 8 chs: 9 sc.
Row 2: Ch 1, turn; sc in each sc across.
Repeat Row 2, 7(9) times; at end of last row, finish off.

SIDES

Row 1: With **right** side facing and working in free loops of beginning ch, join yarn with slip st in first ch, ch 1, sc in same st and in next 10 chs, working in ends of rows along Instep, work 8(10) sc evenly spaced across, sc in each sc across last row of Instep, working in ends of rows along second side of Instep, work 8(10) sc evenly spaced across, working in free loops of beginning ch, sc in next 11 chs: 47(51) sc.

Size Newborn to 3 months ONLY
Rows 2 and 3: Ch 1, turn; sc in each sc across.
Row 4: Ch 1, turn; sc in first 18 sc, [pull up a loop in each of next 2 sc, YO and draw through all 3 loops on hook **(decrease made)]**, sc in next 7 sc, decrease, sc in each sc across: 45 sc.
Row 5: Ch 1, turn; sc in each sc across.
Row 6: Ch 1, turn; sc in first 18 sc, decrease, sc in next 5 sc, decrease, sc in each sc across: 43 sc.
Row 7: Ch 1, turn; sc in each sc across.
Row 8: Ch 1, turn; sc in first 18 sc, decrease, sc in next 3 sc, decrease, sc in each sc across: 41 sc.
Row 9: Ch 1, turn; sc in each sc across; do **not** finish off.

Size 4 to 6 months ONLY
Rows 2-4: Ch 1, turn; sc in each sc across.
Row 5: Ch 1, turn; sc in first 20 sc, [pull up a loop in each of next 2 sc, YO and draw through all 3 loops on hook **(decrease made)]**, sc in next 7 sc, decrease, sc in each sc across: 49 sc.
Rows 6 and 7: Ch 1, turn; sc in each sc across.
Row 8: Ch 1, turn; sc in first 20 sc, decrease, sc in next 5 sc, decrease, sc in each sc across: 47 sc.
Rows 9 and 10: Ch 1, turn; sc in each sc across.
Row 11: Ch 1, turn; sc in first 20 sc, decrease, sc in next 3 sc, decrease, sc in each sc across: 45 sc.
Row 12: Sc in each sc across; do **not** finish off.

FINISHING

With **right** sides together, fold Bootie in half; working through **both** thicknesses, slip st in each sc across bottom; finish off. Sew back seam.
Weave Ribbon through Row 1 of Cuff.

EDGING

With **right** side facing, join pearl cotton with slip st in dc before any Shell, ★ 9 dc in next ch-2 sp, skip 2 dc, slip st in next dc, skip 2 dc, 7 dc in next dc, skip 2 dc, slip st in next dc; repeat from ★ 2 times **more**; finish off.

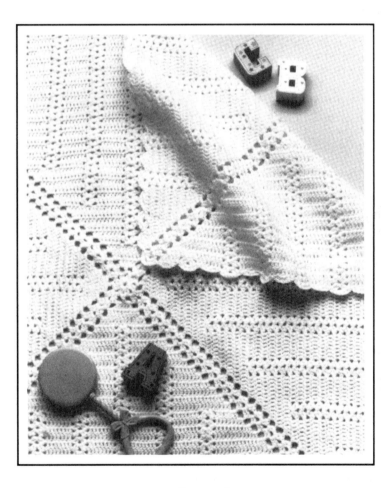

BLANKET to Crochet

Size: Approximately 32" x 32"

MATERIALS

Baby Yarn, approximately:
9 ounces, (260 grams, 1,575 yards)
Size 8 Pearl Cotton (for Edging), approximately 75 yards
Crochet hook, size D (3.00 mm) **or** size needed for gauge

GAUGE: (7 dc, Shell) twice = 4"